Excel® 2010
FOR
DUMMIES®
MINI EDITION

by Greg Harvey, PhD

WILEY

Wiley Publishing, Inc.

Excel® 2010 For Dummies,® Mini Edition

Published by
Wiley Publishing, Inc.
111 River Street
Hoboken, NJ 07030-5774
www.wiley.com

Copyright © 2011 by Wiley Publishing, Inc., Indianapolis, Indiana

Published by Wiley Publishing, Inc., Indianapolis, Indiana

Published simultaneously in Canada

For general information on our other products and services, please contact our Customer Care Department within the U.S. at 877-762-2974, outside the U.S. at 317-572-3993, or fax 317-572-4002.

For technical support, please visit www.wiley.com/techsupport.

Wiley also publishes its books in a variety of electronic formats. Some content that appears in print may not be available in electronic books.

ISBN: 978-1-118-07477-0

Manufactured in the United States of America

WILEY

Contents at a Glance

Publisher's Acknowledgments

We're proud of this book; please send us your comments through our online registration form located at http://dummies.custhelp.com.

Some of the people who helped bring this book to market include the following:

Acquisitions and Editorial

Project Editors: Kim Darosett, Nicole Sholly

Senior Acquisitions Editor: Katie Feltman

Copy Editor: Brian Walls

Composition Services

Project Coordinator: Kristie Rees

Layout and Graphics: Erin Zeltner

Proofreader: Susan Moritz

Publishing and Editorial for Technology Dummies

Richard Swadley, Vice President and Executive Group Publisher

Andy Cummings, Vice President and Publisher

Mary Bednarek, Executive Acquisitions Director

Mary C. Corder, Editorial Director

Publishing for Consumer Dummies

Diane Graves Steele, Vice President and Publisher

Composition Services

Debbie Stailey, Director of Composition Services

Introduction

● ●

I'm very proud to present you with *Excel 2010 For Dummies,* Mini Edition. This book covers cover such fundamentals as how to start the program, identify the parts of the screen, enter information in the worksheet, save a document, and so on.

About This Book

Each discussion of a topic briefly addresses the question of what a particular feature is good for before launching into how to use it. In Excel, as with most other sophisticated programs, you usually have more than one way to do a task. For the sake of your sanity, I have purposely limited the choices by usually giving you only the most efficient ways to do a particular task. Later, if you're so tempted, you can experiment with alternative ways of doing a task. For now, just concentrate on performing the task as I describe.

I'm going to make only one assumption about you (let's see how close I get): You have access to a PC (at least some of the time) that is running Windows 7, Windows Vista, or Windows XP and on which Microsoft Office Excel 2010 is installed. Having said that, I don't assume that you've ever launched Excel 2010, let alone done anything with it.

Conventions Used in This Book

Throughout the book, you'll find Ribbon command sequences (the name on the tab on the Ribbon and the command button you select) separated by a command arrow, as in:

Home⇨Copy

This shorthand is the Ribbon command that copies whatever cells or graphics are currently selected to the Windows Clipboard. It means that you click the Home tab on the Ribbon (if it isn't displayed already) and then click the Copy button (which sports the traditional side-by-side page icon).

Icons Used in This Book

The following icons are placed in the margins to point out stuff you may or may not want to read.

This icon alerts you to shortcuts or other valuable hints related to the topic at hand.

This icon alerts you to information to keep in mind if you want to meet with a modicum of success.

Part I

The Excel 2010 User Experience

• •

In This Part

▶ Getting familiar with the program window

▶ Selecting commands from the Ribbon

▶ Starting and quitting Excel

▶ Getting some help

▶ Finding out what's cool in Excel 2010

• •

The Excel 2010 user interface, like Excel 2007, scraps its reliance on a series of pull-down menus, task panes, and multitudinous toolbars. Instead, it uses a single strip at the top of the worksheet called the Ribbon that puts the bulk of the Excel commands you use at your fingertips at all times.

Add to the Ribbon a File tab and a Quick Access toolbar — along with a few remaining task panes (Clipboard, Clip Art, and Research) — and you end up with the handiest way to crunch your numbers, produce and print polished financial reports, as well as organize and chart your data. In other words, do all the wonderful things for which you rely on Excel.

This part breaks down the Excel user interface and helps you make sense of the tabs and command buttons you're going to face day after day. If you run into trouble, I show you how to get help within Excel. Finally, I give you a rundown of the top ten features in Excel 2010.

Excel's Ribbon User Interface

When you launch Excel 2010, the program opens the first of three new worksheets (named Sheet1) in a new workbook file (named Book1) inside a program window like the one shown in Figure 1-1.

The Excel program window containing this worksheet of the workbook contains the following components:

- ✓ **File tab** that when clicked opens the new Backstage View — a menu on the left that contains all the document- and file-related commands, including Info (selected by default), Save, Save As, Open, Close, Recent, New, Print, and Save & Send. Additionally, there's a Help option with add-ins, an Options item that enables you to change many of Excel's default settings, and an Exit option to quit the program.

- ✓ Customizable **Quick Access toolbar** that contains buttons you can click to perform common tasks, such as saving your work and undoing and redoing edits.

✔ **Ribbon** that contains the bulk of the Excel commands arranged into a series of tabs ranging from Home through View.

✔ **Formula bar** that displays the address of the current cell along with the contents of that cell.

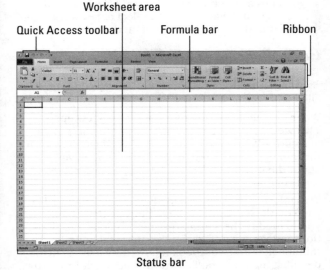

Worksheet area

Quick Access toolbar | Formula bar | Ribbon

Status bar

Figure 1-1: The Excel 2010 program window that appears immediately after launching the program.

- ✔ **Worksheet area** that contains the cells of the worksheet identified by column headings using letters along the top and row headings using numbers along the left edge, tabs for selecting new worksheets, a horizontal scroll bar to move left and right through the sheet, and a vertical scroll bar to move up and down through the sheet.

- ✔ **Status bar** that keeps you informed of the program's current mode and any special keys you engage and enables you to select a new worksheet view and to zoom in and out on the worksheet.

Going Backstage via File

To the immediate left of the Home tab on the Ribbon right below the Quick Access toolbar, you find the File tab.

When you click File, the new Backstage View opens. This view contains a menu similar to the one shown in Figure 1-2. When you open the Backstage View with the Info option selected, Excel displays at-a-glance stats about the workbook file you have open and active in the program.

This information panel is divided into two panes. The pane on the left contains large buttons that enable you to modify the workbook's permissions, distribution, and versions. The pane on the right contains a thumbnail of the workbook followed by a list of fields detailing the workbook's various Document Properties, some of which you can change (such as Title, Tags, Categories, and Author), and many of which you can't (such as Size, Last Modified, Created, and so forth).

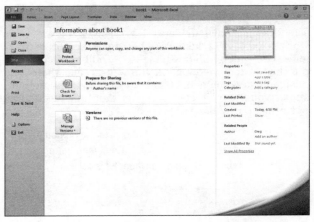

Figure 1-2: Open Backstage View to get at-a-glance information about the current file.

Above the Info option, you find the commands (Save, Save As, Open, and Close) you commonly need for working with Excel workbook files. Near the bottom, the File tab contains a Help option that, when selected, displays a Support panel in the Backstage View. This panel contains options for getting help on using Excel, customizing its default settings, as well as checking for updates to the Excel 2010 program. Below Help, you find options that you can select to change the program's settings, along with an Exit option that you can select when you're ready to close the program.

Bragging about the Ribbon

The Ribbon (shown in Figure 1-3) changes the way you work in Excel 2010. Instead of having to memorize (or guess) on which pull-down menu or toolbar Microsoft put the particular command you want to use, their designers and engineers came up with the Ribbon that shows you the most commonly used options needed to perform a particular Excel task.

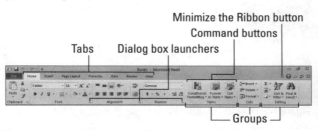

Figure 1-3: The Ribbon consists of a series of tabs containing command buttons arranged into different groups.

The Ribbon contains the following components:

- ✔ **Tabs** for each of Excel's main tasks that bring together and display all the commands commonly needed to perform that core task.

- ✔ **Groups** that organize related command buttons into subtasks normally performed as part of the tab's larger core task.

- ✔ **Command buttons** within each group that you select to perform a particular action or to open a gallery from which you can click a particular

thumbnail. *Note:* Many command buttons on
certain tabs of the Ribbon are organized into
minitoolbars with related settings.

✔ **Dialog box launcher** in the lower-right corner of
certain groups that opens a dialog box containing
a bunch of additional options you can select.

 To display more of the Worksheet area in
the program window, you can minimize the
Ribbon so that only its tabs display. Simply
click the Minimize the Ribbon button, shown
in Figure 1-3.

The most direct method for selecting commands on the
Ribbon is to click the tab that contains the command
button you want and then click that button in its group.
For example, to insert a piece of clip art into your
spreadsheet, you click the Insert tab and then click the
Clip Art button to open the Clip Art task pane in the
Worksheet area.

Having fun with the Formula bar

The Formula bar displays the cell address (determined
by a column letter(s) followed by a row number) and
the contents of the current cell. (Refer to Figure 1-1.)
For example, cell A1 is the first cell of each worksheet
at the intersection of column A and row 1; cell
XFD1048576 is the last cell of each worksheet at the
intersection of column XFD and row 1048576. The type
of entry you make determines the contents of the current cell: text or numbers, for example, if you enter a
heading or particular value, or the details of a formula
if you enter a calculation.

The Formula bar has three sections:

- ✔ **Name box:** The left-most section that displays the address of the current cell.

- ✔ **Formula bar buttons:** The second, middle section that appears as a rather nondescript button displaying only an indented circle on the left (used to narrow or widen the Name box) and the Insert Function button (labeled *fx*) on the right. When you start making or editing a cell entry, Cancel (an X) and Enter (a check mark) buttons appear between them.

- ✔ **Cell contents:** The third, right-most white area to the immediate right of the Insert Function button takes up the rest of the bar and expands as necessary to display really long cell entries that won't fit in the normal area.

What to do in the Worksheet area

The Worksheet area is where most of the Excel spreadsheet action takes place because it's the place that displays the cells in different sections of the current worksheet, and it's right inside the cells that you do all your spreadsheet data entry and formatting in, not to mention a great deal of your editing.

To enter or edit data in a cell, that cell must be current. Excel indicates that a cell is current in three ways:

- ✔ The cell cursor — the dark black border surrounding the cell's entire perimeter — appears in the cell.

- ✔ The address of the cell appears in the Name box of the Formula bar.

✔ The cell's column letter(s) and row number are shaded (in kind of an orange-beige color on most monitors) in the column headings and row headings that appear at the top and left of the Worksheet area, respectively.

An Excel worksheet contains far too many columns and rows for all of a worksheet's cells to be displayed at one time regardless of how large your screen is or how high the screen resolution. Therefore, Excel offers many methods for moving the cell cursor around the worksheet to the cell where you want to enter new data or edit existing data:

✔ Click the desired cell — assuming that the cell is displayed within the section of the sheet visible in the Worksheet area.

✔ Click the Name box, type the address of the desired cell, and then press the Enter key.

✔ Use the cursor keys to move the cell cursor to the desired cell.

✔ Use the horizontal and vertical scroll bars at the bottom and right edge of the Worksheet area to move to the part of the worksheet that contains the desired cell and then click the cell to put the cell cursor in it.

On the left side of the bottom of the Worksheet area, the Sheet Tab scroll buttons appear, followed by the actual tabs for the worksheets in your workbook and the Insert Worksheet button. (See Figure 1-4.) To activate a worksheet for editing, you select it by clicking its sheet tab. Excel lets you know what sheet is active by displaying the sheet name in boldface type and making its tab appear on top of the others.

First sheet

Previous sheet

Next sheet

Last sheet

Current sheet

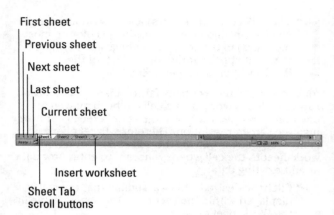

Insert worksheet

Sheet Tab
scroll buttons

Figure 1-4: These buttons enable you to activate your work-sheets and add to them.

Launching and Quitting Excel

You can launch Excel from the Windows Start menu by choosing Start➪All Programs➪Microsoft Office➪ Microsoft Excel 2010.

When you're ready to call it a day and quit Excel, choose File➪Exit or click the Close button (the X) in the upper-right corner of the program window.

If you try to exit Excel after working on a workbook and you haven't saved your latest changes, the program displays an alert box asking whether you want to save your changes. To save your changes before exiting, click the Save command button. If you've just been playing around in the worksheet and don't want to save your changes, you can abandon the document by clicking the Don't Save button.

Help Is on the Way

You can get online help with Excel 2010 anytime that you need it while using the program. Simply click the Help button (the button with the question mark icon to the immediate right of the Minimize the Ribbon button on the right side of the program window) or press F1 to open a separate Excel Help window. (See Figure 1-5.)

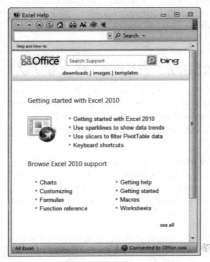

Figure 1-5: The Excel Help window automatically connects you to the Internet when you open it.

When the Excel Help window opens, Excel attempts to use your Internet connection to update its topics. The opening Help window contains links that you can click to get information on what's new in the program.

To get help with a particular command or function, use the Search box at the top of the Excel Help window. Type keywords or a phrase describing your topic (such as "print preview" or "printing worksheets") in this text box and press Enter. The Excel Help window then presents a list of links to related help topics that you can click to display the information.

To display a table of contents with all the main categories and subtopics arranged hierarchically, click the Show Table of Contents button (with the book icon) on the toolbar.

Top Ten Features in Excel 2010

If you're looking for a quick rundown on what's cool in Excel 2010, look no further! Here it is — my official Top Ten Features list. Just a cursory glance down the list tells you that the thrust of the features is graphics, graphics, graphics!

- ✔ **Live Preview:** You simply can't say enough about Live Preview, including how much easier it makes formatting the worksheet. Live Preview works with all the style galleries as well as Font and Font Size drop-down menus in the Font group on the Home tab. It enables you to see how the data in the current cell selection would look with a particular formatting, font, or font size before you actually apply the formatting to the range.

✔ **The Ribbon:** The Ribbon is the heart of the new Excel 2010 user interface. Based on a core of standard tabs to which various so-called contextual tabs are added as needed in formatting and editing of specific elements (such as data tables, charts, pivot tables, and graphic objects), the Ribbon brings together most every command you're going to need when performing particular tasks in Excel. (See "Excel's Ribbon User Interface," earlier in this part.)

✔ **Document Information and Printing in Backstage View:** The brand-new Backstage View in Excel enables you to get all the properties and stats (technically known as metadata) about the workbook file you're editing on one pane simply by choosing File➪Info. This new Backstage View also makes it a breeze to preview, change settings, and print your worksheet using its new Print panel. (See the earlier section "Going Backstage via File" for more on getting at-a-glance information about your document in the Backstage View. See Part III for details on printing the worksheet using the new Print panel.)

✔ **Style galleries:** Excel 2010 is jammed full of style galleries that make it a snap to apply new sophisticated formatting to the charts, tables, and lists of data, and various and sundry graphics that you add to your worksheets. Coupled with the Live Preview feature, Excel's style galleries go a long way toward encouraging you to create better looking, more colorful, and interesting spreadsheets.

✔ **Page Layout View:** Page Layout View is just what the doctor ordered when it comes to visualizing the paging of printed reports. When you turn on this view by clicking the Page Layout View button on the Status bar, Excel doesn't just show the page breaks as measly dotted lines as in earlier versions but as actual separations. Additionally, the program shows the margins for each page, including headers and footers defined for the report (which you can both define and edit directly in the margin areas while the program is in this view). (See Part III for more on this feature.)

- **Format As Table:** This feature is a real keeper. By formatting a table of data with one of the many table styles available on the Table Styles drop-down gallery, you're assured that all new entries made to the table are going to be formatted in the same manner as others in similar positions in the table. Better yet, all new entries to the table are considered part of the table automatically when it comes to formatting, sorting, and filtering.

- **Charts from the Insert tab:** Excel 2010, like its immediate predecessor, retires the Chart Wizard and offers you direct access to all the major types of charts on the Ribbon's Insert tab. Simply select the data to chart, click the command button for the chart type on the Insert tab, and then select the style you want for that chart type.

- **Formatting and editing from the Home tab:** The Home tab of the Excel Ribbon literally brings home all the commonly used formatting and editing features. Gone are the days when you had to fish for the right button on some long, drawn-out toolbar or on some partially deployed pull-down menu. Now all you have to do is find the group that holds the command button you need and click it. (See Part II for more on formatting cells.)

- ✔ **Cell styles:** Excel 2010 has more than 40 colorful ready-made styles. You can preview these styles in the worksheet with Live Preview to see how they look on the data before you apply them. You apply a cell style to the cell selection by quickly and easily clicking its thumbnail in the Cells Styles gallery. You can open this gallery by clicking the Cell Styles button in the Styles group on the Home tab.

- ✔ **Conditional formatting and sparklines:** Conditional formatting in Excel 2010 gives you the ability to define formatting when the values in cells meet certain conditions. You can now instantly apply one of many different Data Bars, Color Scales, and Icon Sets to the cell selection merely by clicking the set's thumbnail in the respective pop-up palettes.

  Sparklines are the newest graphic addition to Excel. They are tiny charts (so small they fit within the current height of a worksheet cell) that visually represent changes in ranges of associated data. You can use sparklines to call attention to trends in the data as well as to help your users quickly spot high and low values.

Part II

Creating and Editing Spreadsheets

. . . .

In This Part

▶ Entering data in a worksheet

▶ Creating simple formulas

▶ Using AutoFill to create a series of entries

▶ Selecting and formatting cells

▶ Adjusting column width and row height

▶ Saving your work

. . . .

After you know how to launch Excel 2010, it's time to find out how not to get yourself into trouble when actually using it! In this part, you find out how to put all kinds of information into those little, blank worksheet cells I describe in Part I. You also discover how to select and format cells as well as adjust column width and row height.

After discovering how to fill up a worksheet with raw data, you find out what has to be the most important lesson of all — how to save all that information on disk so that you don't ever have to enter the stuff again.

Doing the Data-Entry Thing

When you start Excel without specifying a document to open, you get a blank workbook in a new workbook window. This workbook, temporarily named Book1, contains three blank worksheets (Sheet1, Sheet2, and Sheet3). To begin to work on a new spreadsheet, you position the cell pointer in the cell where you want the data and then begin typing the entry.

When you start typing, Excel goes through a mode change from Ready to Enter mode (and *Enter* replaces *Ready* as the Program indicator at the far left of the Status bar).

If you're not in Ready mode, try pressing Esc.

The characters that you type in a cell in the worksheet area simultaneously appear on the Formula bar near the top of the screen. Typing something in the current cell also triggers a change to the Formula bar because two new buttons, Cancel and Enter, appear between the Name box drop-down button and the Insert Function button.

As you continue to type, Excel displays your progress on the Formula bar and in the active cell in the worksheet (see Figure 2-1). However, the insertion point (the flashing vertical bar that acts as your cursor) displays only at the end of the characters displayed in the cell.

After you finish typing your cell entry, you still have to get it into the cell so that it stays put. To complete your cell entry and, at the same time, get Excel out of Enter

mode and back into Ready mode, press the Enter key
or press one of the arrow keys (↓, ↑, →, or ←) to move
to another cell.

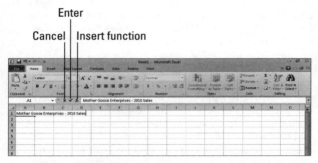

Figure 2-1: What you type appears both in the current cell and
on the Formula bar.

As soon as you complete your entry in the current cell,
Excel deactivates the Formula bar by removing the
Cancel and Enter buttons. Thereafter, the data you
entered continues to appear in the cell in the worksheet, and every time you put the cell pointer into that
cell, the data will reappear on the Formula bar as well.

It Takes All Types

Unbeknownst to you while you go about happily entering data in your spreadsheet, Excel constantly analyzes
the stuff you type and classifies it into one of three possible data types: a piece of *text,* a *value,* or a *formula*.

If Excel finds that the entry is a formula, the program automatically calculates the formula and displays the computed result in the worksheet cell (you continue to see the formula itself, however, on the Formula bar). If Excel is satisfied that the entry does not qualify as a formula, the program then determines whether the entry should be classified as text or as a value.

Excel makes this distinction between text and values so that it knows how to align the entry in the worksheet. It aligns text entries with the left edge of the cell and values with the right edge. Because most formulas work properly only when they are fed values, by differentiating text from values, the program knows which will and will not work in the formulas that you build. Suffice it to say that you can foul up your formulas but good if they refer to any cells containing text where Excel expects values to be.

The telltale signs of text

A text entry is simply an entry that Excel can't pigeonhole as either a formula or value. This makes text the catchall category of Excel data types. As a practical rule, most text entries (also known as *labels*) are a combination of letters and punctuation or letters and numbers. Text is used mostly for titles, headings, and notes in the worksheet.

You can tell right away whether Excel has accepted a cell entry as text because text entries automatically align at the left edge of their cells. If the text entry is wider than the cell can display, the data spills into the neighboring cell or cells on the right, *as long as those cells remain blank* (see Figure 2-2).

A9			▾		*fx*	Little Bo Peep Pet Detectives		
	A	B	C	D	E	F	G	H	I
1	Mother Goose Enterprises - 2010 Sales								
2		Jan	Feb	Mar					
3	Jack Sprat Diet Centers								
4	Jack and Jill Trauma Centers								
5	Mother Hubbard Dog Goodies								
6	Rub-a-Dub-Dub Tubs and Spas								
7	Georgie Porgie Pudding Pies								
8	Hickory, Dickory, Doc Clock Repair								
9	Little Bo Peep Pet Detectives								
10									
11									
12									
13									
14									
15									

Figure 2-2: Long text entries spill over into neighboring blank cells.

If, sometime later, you enter information in a cell that contains spillover text from a cell to its left, Excel cuts off the spillover of the long text entry (see Figure 2-3). Not to worry: Excel doesn't actually lop off these characters — it simply shaves the display to make room for the new entry. To redisplay the seemingly missing portion of the long text entry, you have to widen the column that contains the cell where the text is entered. (To find out how to do this, skip ahead to the section "Adjusting Rows and Columns.")

How Excel evaluates its values

Values are the building blocks of most of the formulas that you create in Excel. As such, values come in two flavors: numbers that represent quantities (*14* stores or *$140,000* dollars) and numbers that represent dates (*July 30, 1995*) or times (*2* p.m.).

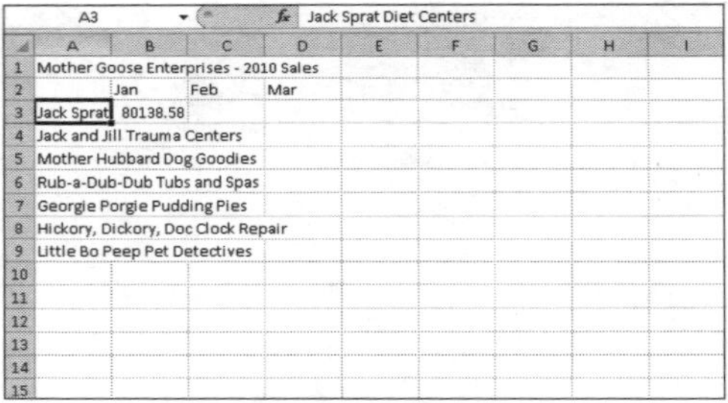

Figure 2-3: Entries in cells to the right cut off the spillover text in cells on the left.

You can tell whether Excel has accepted your entry as a value because values automatically align at the right edge of their cells. If the value that you enter is wider than the column containing the cell can display, Excel automatically converts the value to (of all things) *scientific notation*. To restore a value that's been converted into that weird scientific notation stuff to a regular number, simply widen the column for that cell, as described in the later section, "Adjusting Rows and Columns."

Here are a few tips for entering numbers:

✔ To enter a numeric value that represents a positive quantity, just select a cell, type the numbers — for example, **459600** — and complete the entry in the cell by pressing Enter. To enter a numeric value that represents a negative quantity, begin the entry with the minus sign or hyphen (–) before typing the numbers and then complete the entry. For example, **–175**.

✔ With numeric values that represent dollar amounts, you can include dollar signs ($) and commas (,) just as they appear in the printed or handwritten numbers you're working from.

✔ When entering numeric values with decimal places, use the period as the decimal point. When you enter decimal values, the program automatically adds a zero before the decimal point (Excel inserts 0.34 in a cell when you enter **.34**) and drops trailing zeros entered after the decimal point (Excel inserts 12.5 in a cell when you enter **12.50**).

Fabricating those fabulous formulas!

Formulas are the real workhorses of the worksheet. If you set up a formula properly, it computes the correct answer when you enter the formula into a cell. From then on, the formula stays up to date, recalculating the results whenever you change any of the values that the formula uses.

You let Excel know that you're about to enter a formula (rather than some text or a value) in the current cell by starting the formula with the equal sign (=). Most simple formulas follow the equal sign with a built-in function, such as SUM or AVERAGE. Other simple formulas use a series of values or cell references that contain values separated by one or more of the following mathematical operators:

+ (plus sign) for addition

– (minus sign or hyphen) for subtraction

* (asterisk) for multiplication

/ (slash) for division

^ (caret) for raising a number to an exponential power

For example, to create a formula in cell C2 that multiplies a value entered in cell A2 by a value in cell B2, enter the following formula in cell C2: **=A2*B2**.

To enter this formula in cell C2, type the formula directly in the cell or follow these steps:

1. **Select cell C2.**
2. **Type = (equal sign).**
3. **Select cell A2.**

   This action places the cell reference A2 in the formula in the cell (as shown in Figure 2-4).

TRANSPOSE	▾	✕ ✓ ƒx	=A2			
	A	**B**	**C**	**D**	**E**	**F**	**G**
1						
2	20	100	=A2			
3						
4						
5						

Figure 2-4: To start the formula, type = and then select cell A2.

4. **Type * (an asterisk).**

   The asterisk is used for multiplication rather than the × symbol you used in school.

5. **Select cell B2.**

   This action places the cell reference B2 in the formula (as shown in Figure 2-5).

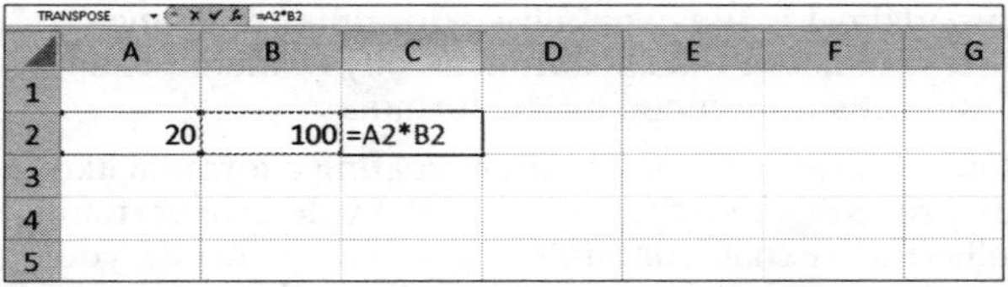

	A	B	C	D	E	F	G
1							
2	20	100	=A2*B2				
3							
4							
5							

TRANSPOSE ▾ (× ✓ *fx* =A2*B2

Figure 2-5: To complete the second part of the formula, type *
and select cell B2.

6. **Click the Enter button to complete the formula
   entry while keeping the cell pointer in cell C2.**

   Excel displays the calculated answer in cell C2
   and the formula =A2*B2 in the Formula bar (as
   shown in Figure 2-6).

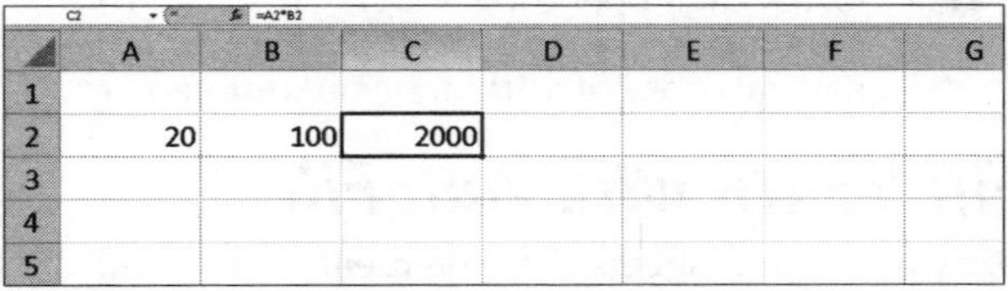

C2 ▾ (*fx* =A2*B2

	A	B	C	D	E	F	G
1							
2	20	100	2000				
3							
4							
5							

Figure 2-6: Excel displays the answer in cell C2 while the formula appears in the Formula bar above.

When you finish entering the formula **=A2*B2** in cell
C2 of the worksheet, Excel displays the calculated
result, depending on the values currently entered in
cells A2 and B2. The major strength of the electronic

spreadsheet is the capability of formulas to change their calculated results automatically to match changes in the cells referenced by the formulas.

Now comes the fun part: After creating a formula like the preceding one that refers to the values in certain cells (rather than containing those values itself), you can change the values in those cells, and Excel automatically recalculates the formula using these new values and displays the updated answer in the worksheet. Using the example shown in Figure 2-6, suppose that you change the value in cell B2 from 100 to 50. The moment that you complete this change in cell B2, Excel recalculates the formula and displays the new answer, 1000, in cell C2.

Many formulas that you create perform more than one mathematical operation. Excel performs each operation, moving from left to right, according to a strict pecking order (the natural order of arithmetic operations).

Fill 'er Up with AutoFill

Many of the worksheets that you create with Excel require the entry of a series of sequential dates or numbers. For example, a worksheet may require you to title the columns with the 12 months, from January through December, or to number the rows from 1 to 100.

Excel's AutoFill feature makes short work of this kind of repetitive task. All you have to enter is the starting value for the series. In most cases, AutoFill is smart enough to figure out how to fill out the series for you when you drag the fill handle to the right (to take the series across columns to the right) or down (to extend the series to the rows below).

The AutoFill handle looks like this — + — and appears only when you position the mouse pointer on the lower-right corner of the active cell (or the last cell, when you've selected a block of cells).

When creating a series with the fill handle, you can drag in only one direction at a time. For example, you can fill the series or copy the entry to the range to the left or right of the cell that contains the initial values, or you can fill the series or copy to the range above or below the cell containing the initial values.

While you drag the mouse, the program keeps you informed of whatever entry will be entered into the last cell selected in the range by displaying that entry next to the mouse pointer (a kind of AutoFill tips, if you will). When you release the mouse button after extending the range with the fill handle, Excel either creates a series in all the cells that you selected or copies the entire range with the initial value. To the right of the last entry in the filled or copied series, Excel also displays a drop-down button that contains a shortcut menu of options that enable you to override Excel's default filling or copying.

In Figures 2-7 and 2-8, I illustrate how to use AutoFill to enter a row of months, starting with January in cell B2 and ending with June in cell G2. To do this, you simply enter **January** in cell B2 and then position the mouse

pointer on the fill handle in the lower-right corner of
this cell before you drag through to cell G2 on the right
(as shown in Figure 2-7).

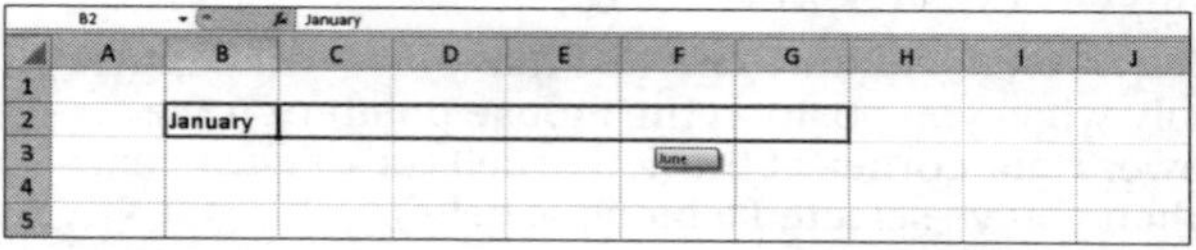

Figure 2-7: Enter the first month and then drag the Fill handle in
a direction to add sequential months.

When you release the mouse button, Excel fills in the
names of the rest of the months (February through
June) in the selected cells (as shown in Figure 2-8).
Excel keeps the cells with the series of months
selected, giving you another chance to modify the
series. (If you went too far, you can drag the fill handle
to the left to cut back on the list of months; if you
didn't go far enough, you can drag it to the right to
extend the list of months further.)

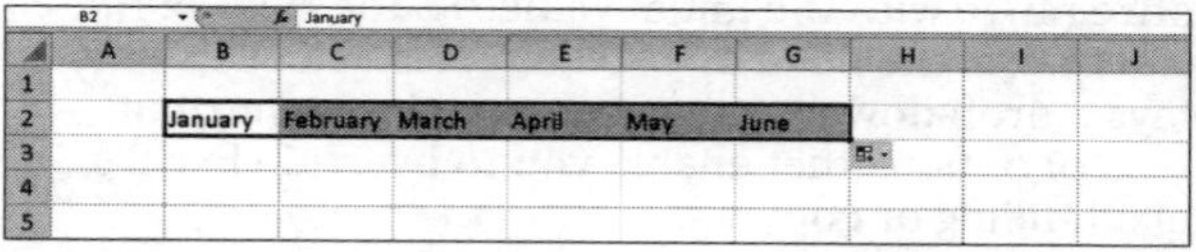

Figure 2-8: Release the mouse button, and Excel fills the cell
selection with the missing months.

Also, you can use the options on the AutoFill Options drop-down menu (opened by clicking the drop-down button that appears on the fill handle to the right of June) to override the series created by default. For example, to have Excel copy January into each of the selected cells, choose Copy Cells on this menu.

Choosing a Select Group of Cells

Given the monotonously rectangular nature of the worksheet and its components, it shouldn't come as a surprise to find that all the cell selections you make in the worksheet have the same kind of cubist feel to them. After all, worksheets are just blocks of cells of varying numbers of columns and rows.

A *cell selection* (or *cell range*) is whatever collection of neighboring cells you choose to format or edit. The smallest possible cell selection in a worksheet is just one cell: the so-called *active cell*. The cell with the cell cursor is really just a single cell selection. The largest possible cell selection in a worksheet is all the cells in that worksheet (the whole enchilada, so to speak). Most of the cell selections you need for formatting a worksheet will probably fall somewhere in between, consisting of cells in several adjacent columns and rows.

Excel shows a cell selection in the worksheet by highlighting in color the entire block of cells within the extended cell cursor except for the active cell that keeps its original color. (Figure 2-9 shows several cell selections of different sizes and shapes.)

In Excel, you can select more than one cell range at a time (a phenomenon somewhat ingloriously called a *noncontiguous* or *nonadjacent selection*). In fact, although Figure 2-9 appears to contain several cell selections, it's really just one big, nonadjacent cell selection with cell D12 (the active one) as the cell that was selected last.

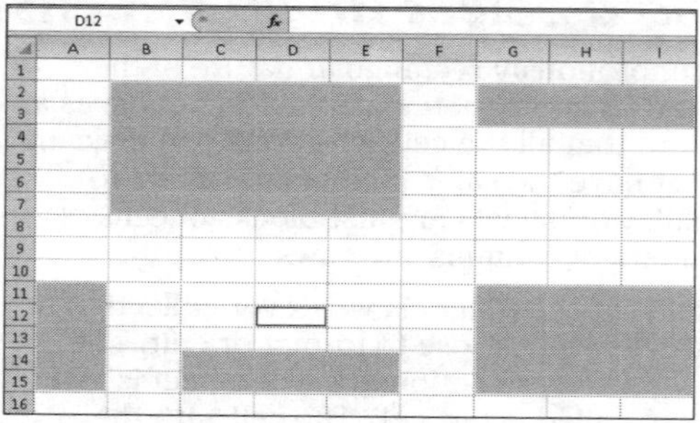

Figure 2-9: Cell selections of various shapes and sizes.

Point-and-click cell selections

The mouse is a natural for selecting a range of cells. Just position the mouse pointer (in its thick, white cross form) on the first cell and then click and drag in the direction that you want to extend the selection.

✔ To extend the cell selection to columns to the right, drag your mouse to the right, highlighting neighboring cells as you go.

- ✔ To extend the selection to rows to the bottom, drag your mouse down.

- ✔ To extend the selection down and to the right at the same time, drag your mouse diagonally toward the cell in the lower-right corner of the block you're highlighting.

Keyboard cell selections

If you're not keen on using the mouse, you can use the keyboard to select the cells you want. Sticking with the Shift+click method of selecting cells, the easiest way to select cells with the keyboard is to combine the Shift key with other keystrokes that move the cell cursor.

Start by positioning the cell cursor in the first cell of the selection and then holding the Shift key while you press the appropriate cell-pointer movement keys. When you hold the Shift key while you press direction keys — such as the arrow keys (↑, →, ↓, ←), PgUp, or PgDn — Excel anchors the selection on the current cell, moves the cell cursor, and highlights cells as it goes.

When making a cell selection this way, you can continue to alter the size and shape of the cell range with the cell-pointer movement keys as long as you don't release the Shift key. After you release the Shift key, pressing any of the cell-pointer movement keys immediately collapses the selection, reducing it to just the cell with the cell cursor.

Formatting Cells

Excel offers a number of different ways that you can format cells. In the following sections, I discuss how to format data tables with the Format as Table feature and how to use the cell formatting buttons on the Home tab.

Having fun with the Format as Table Gallery

Here's a formatting technique that doesn't require you to do any prior cell selecting. (Kinda figures, doesn't it?) The Format as Table feature is so automatic that the cell cursor just has to be within the table of data prior to your clicking the Format as Table command button in the Styles group on the Home tab. Clicking the Format as Table command button opens its rather extensive Table gallery with the formatting thumbnails divided into three sections — Light, Medium, and Dark — each of which describes the intensity of the colors used by its various formats.

As soon as you click one of the table formatting thumbnails in this Table gallery, Excel makes its best guess as to the cell range of the data table to apply it to (indicated by the marquee around its perimeter), and the Format As Table dialog box, similar to the one shown in Figure 2-10, appears.

This dialog box contains a Where Is the Data for Your Table text box that shows the address of the cell range currently selected by the marquee and a My Table Has Headers check box.

If Excel does not correctly guess the range of the data table you want to format, drag through the cell range to adjust the marquee and the range address in the Where Is the Data for Your Table text box. If your data table doesn't use column headers or, if the table has them, but you still don't want Excel to add Filter drop-down buttons to each column heading, deselect the My Table Has Headers check box.

	A	B	C	D	E	F	G	H	I	J
	A3	▾	f_x	Part No.						
1	**Production Schedule for 2010**									
2										
3	Part No.	Apr-10	May-10	Jun-10	Jul-10	Aug-10	Sep-10	Oct-10	Nov-10	Dec-10
4	Part 100	500	485	438	505	483	540	441	550	345
5	Part 101	175	170	153	177	169	189	154	193	200
6	Part 102	350	340	306	354	338	378	309	385	350
7	Part 103	890	863	779	899	859	961	785	979	885
8	Total	1915	1858	1676	1934	1848	2068	1689	2107	1780
9										
10						Format As Table				
11						Where is the data for your table?				
12										
13						☑ My table has headers				
14						OK	Cancel			
15										
16										
17										

Figure 2-10: Selecting a format from the Table gallery and indicating its range in the Format As Table dialog box.

After you click OK, Excel applies the format of the thumbnail you clicked in the gallery to the data table. Additionally, the Design tab appears under the Table Tools contextual tab at the end of the Ribbon, as shown in Figure 2-11.

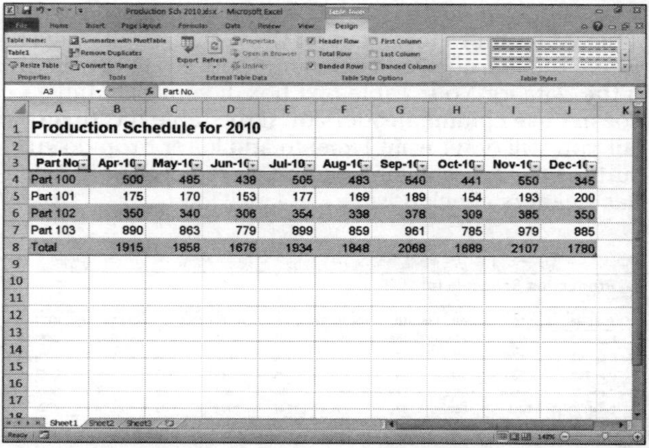

Figure 2-11: After you select a format from the Table gallery, the Design tab appears under the Table Tools contextual tab.

> 💡 The Design tab enables you to use Live Preview to see how your table would appear. Simply position the mouse pointer over any of the format thumbnails in the Table Styles group to see the data in your table appear in that table format.

Cell formatting from the Home tab

Some spreadsheet tables or ranges within them require a lighter touch than the Format as Table command button offers. For example, you may have a data table

where the only emphasis you want to add is to make
the column headings bold at the top of the table and
to underline the row of totals at the bottom (done by
drawing a borderline along the bottom of the cells).

The formatting buttons that appear in the Font,
Alignment, and Number groups on the Home tab
enable you to accomplish just this kind of targeted
cell formatting. Figures 2-12, 2-13, and 2-14 identify
all the formatting buttons in these three groups on
the Home tab.

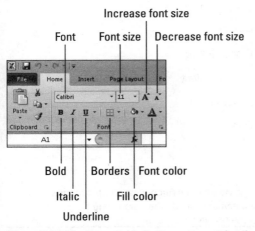

Figure 2-12: The Home tab's Font group contains the tools
you commonly need when modifying the appearance
of the text in a cell range.

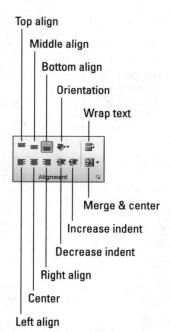

Top align

Middle align

Bottom align

Orientation

Wrap text

Merge & center

Increase indent

Decrease indent

Right align

Center

Left align

Figure 2-13: The Home tab's Alignment group contains the tools you commonly need when modifying the placement of the text in a cell range.

Number format

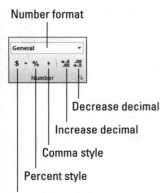

Decrease decimal

Increase decimal

Comma style

Percent style

Accounting number format

Figure 2-14: The Home tab's Number group contains the tools you commonly need when modifying the number format of the values in a cell range.

Adjusting Rows and Columns

For those times when Excel 2010 doesn't automatically adjust the width of your columns to your complete satisfaction, you can use the AutoFit feature. With this method, Excel automatically determines how much to widen or narrow the column to fit the longest entry currently in the column.

Here's how to use AutoFit to get the best fit for a column:

1. **Position the mouse pointer on the right border of the worksheet frame with the column letter at the top of the worksheet.**

   The mouse pointer changes to a double-headed arrow pointing left and right.

2. **Double-click the mouse button.**

   Excel widens or narrows the column width to suit the longest entry.

You can apply a best-fit to more than one column at a time. Simply select all the columns that need adjusting (if the columns neighbor one another, drag through their column letters on the frame; if they don't, hold down the Ctrl key while you click the individual column letters). After you select the columns, double-click any of the right borders on the frame.

The story with adjusting the heights of rows is pretty much the same as that with adjusting columns except that you do a lot less row adjusting than you do column adjusting. That's because Excel automatically changes the height of the rows to accommodate changes to their entries, such as selecting a larger font size or wrapping text in a cell. To use AutoFit to best-fit the entries in a row, you double-click the bottom row-frame border.

Best-fit à la AutoFit doesn't always produce the expected results. For example, a long title that spills into several columns to the right produces a very wide column when you use best-fit. When AutoFit's best-fit won't do, you can adjust column width or row height manually, as described in the following sections.

Adjusting column width manually

To adjust column width manually, drag the right border of the column (on the frame) until it's the size you need. This manual technique for calibrating the column width also works when more than one column is selected. Just be aware that all selected columns assume whatever size you make the one that you're actually dragging.

You can also set the widths of columns from the Format button's drop-down list in the Cells group on the Home tab. When you click this drop-down button, the Cell Size section of this drop-down menu contains the following width options:

- ✔ **Column Width** to open the Column Width dialog box where you enter the number of characters that you want for the column width before you click OK

- ✔ **AutoFit Column Width** to have Excel apply best-fit to the columns based on the widest entries in the current cell selection

- ✔ **Default Width** to open the Standard Width dialog box containing the standard column width of 8.43 characters that you can apply to the columns in the cell selection

Adjusting row height manually

Most row-height adjustments come about when you want to increase the amount of space between a table title and the table or between a row of column headings and the table of information without actually adding a blank row.

To increase the height of a row, drag the bottom border of the row frame down until the row is high enough and then release the mouse button. To shorten a row, reverse this process and drag the bottom row-frame border up. As with columns, you can also adjust the height of selected rows using row options in the Cell Size section on the Format button's drop-down menu on the Home tab:

- ✔ **Row Height** to open the Row Height dialog box where you enter the number of points in the Row Height text box and then click OK

- ✔ **AutoFit Row Height** to return the height of selected rows to the best fit

Making Sure That the Data Is Safe and Sound

All the work you do in any of the worksheets in your workbook is at risk until you save the workbook as a disk file, normally on your computer's hard drive.

When you click the Save button on the Quick Access toolbar (the one with the picture of a 3¼" floppy disk) or choose File⇨Save for the first time, Excel displays the Save As dialog box. Use this dialog box to replace the temporary document name (Book1, Book2, and so forth) with a more descriptive filename in the File Name text box, select a file format in the Save As Type drop-down list box, and select a new drive and folder before you save the workbook as a disk file.

When you finish making changes in the Save As dialog box, click the Save button. When Excel saves your workbook file, the program saves all the information in every worksheet in your workbook (including the last position of the cell cursor) in the designated folder and drive.

Part III

Previewing and Printing

. . . .

In This Part

▶ Previewing pages in Page Layout View

▶ Printing from the Print panel

▶ Fine-tuning your page settings

▶ Adding a header and footer to a report

▶ Fixing page break problems

. . . .

*I*n this part, you find out just how easy it is to print reports with Excel 2010. Thanks to the program's new Print panel in Backstage View, its Page Layout worksheet view, and its handy Page Layout tab on the Ribbon, you can produce top-notch reports the first time you send your document to the printer.

Taking a Gander at the Pages in Page Layout View

Excel 2010's Page Layout View gives you instant access to the paging of the current worksheet. Activate this feature by clicking the Page Layout View command button on the Ribbon's View tab. When you switch to

Page Layout View, Excel adds horizontal and vertical rulers to the column letter and row number headings, as shown in Figure 3-1. In the Worksheet area, this view shows the margins for each printed page, any headers and footers defined for the report, and the breaks between each page.

To see all the pages in the active worksheet, drag the slider button in the Zoom slider to the left until you decrease the screen magnification sufficiently to display all the pages of data.

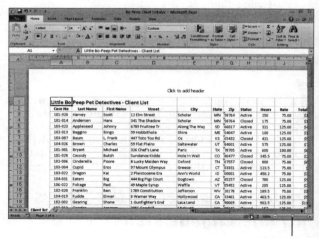

Zoom slider

Figure 3-1: Viewing a spreadsheet in Page Layout View.

Checking and Printing a Report from the Print Panel

To save wasted paper and your sanity, print your worksheet directly from the Print panel in Backstage View by choosing File➪Print. As you see in Figure 3-2, the Print panel shows your current print settings along with a preview of the first page of the printout.

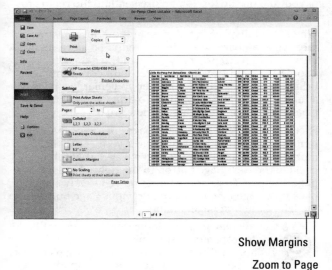

Show Margins

Zoom to Page

Figure 3-2: The Print panel in Backstage View shows your current print settings plus a preview of the printout.

You can use the Print Preview feature in the Print panel before you print any worksheet, section of worksheet, or entire workbook. Because of the peculiarities in paging worksheet data, you often need to check the page breaks for any report that requires more than one page. The print preview area shows you exactly how the worksheet data will page when printed. If necessary, you can return to the worksheet where you can make changes to the page settings from the Page Layout tab on the Ribbon before sending the report to the printer.

When Excel displays a full page in the print preview area, you can barely read its contents. To increase the view to actual size to verify some of the data, click the Zoom to Page button in the lower-right corner of the Print panel (see Figure 3-2). After you enlarge a page to actual size, use the scroll bars to bring new parts of the page into view in the print preview area.

Excel indicates the number of pages in a report at the bottom of the print preview area. If your report has more than one page, you can view pages that follow by clicking the Next Page button to the right of the final page number. To review a page you've already seen, back up a page by clicking the Previous Page button to the left of the first page number.

 To display markers indicating the current left, right, top, and bottom margins along with the column widths, select the Show Margins check box (see Figure 3-2). You can then modify the column widths as well as the page margins by dragging the appropriate marker.

When you finish previewing the report, the Print panel offers you the following options for changing certain print settings before you send it to the printer:

- ✔ **Print** button with the **Number of Copies** combo box: Use this button to print the spreadsheet report using the current print settings listed on the panel. Use the combo box to indicate the number of copies you want to print.

- ✔ **Printer** drop-down button: Use this button to select a new printer or fax to send the spreadsheet report to when more than one device is installed.

- ✔ **Settings** drop-down buttons: Use the Print What drop-down button to choose between printing only the active (selected) worksheets in the workbook (the default), the entire workbook, the current cell selection in the current worksheet, and the currently selected table in the current worksheet. Use the combo boxes to restrict what's printed to just the range of pages you enter in these boxes or select with their spinner buttons.

  Beneath the combo boxes, you find drop-down list buttons to print on both sides of each page in the report, collate the pages of the report, and switch the page orientation from Portrait (aligned with the short side) to Landscape (aligned with the long side). Additionally, you can select a paper size other than the standard 8.5" x 11" letter and customize the size of the report's margins.

My Page Was Set Up!

About the only thing the slightest bit complex in printing a worksheet is figuring out how to get the pages right. Fortunately, the command buttons in the Page Setup group on the Ribbon's Page Layout tab give you a great deal of control over what goes on which page.

Three groups of buttons on the Page Layout tab help you get your page settings exactly as you want them. The Page Setup group, the Scale to Fit group, and the Sheet Options group are described in the following sections.

Using the buttons in the Page Setup group

The Page Setup group of the Page Layout tab contains the following important command buttons:

- ✔ **Margins** button to select one of three preset margins for the report or to set custom margins on the Margins tab of the Page Setup dialog box.

- ✔ **Orientation** button to switch between Portrait and Landscape mode for printing.

- ✔ **Size** button to select one of the preset paper sizes, set a custom size, or change the printing resolution or page number on the Page tab of the Page Setup dialog box.

- ✔ **Print Area** button to set and clear the print area.

- ✔ **Breaks** button to insert or remove page breaks. (See "Solving Page Break Problems" later in this part.)

✔ **Background** button to open the Sheet Background dialog box where you can select a new graphic image or photo to use as a background for the current worksheet.

✔ **Print Titles** button to open the Sheet tab of the Page Setup dialog box where you can define rows of the worksheet to repeat at the top and columns of the worksheet to repeat at the left as print titles for the report.

Using the buttons in the Scale to Fit group

If your printer supports scaling options, you're in luck. You can always get a worksheet to fit on a single page simply by selecting the 1 Page option on the Width and Height drop-down menus attached to their command buttons in the Scale to Fit group on the Ribbon's Page Layout tab. When you select these options, Excel figures out how much to reduce the size of the information you're printing to fit it all on one page.

After clicking the Page Break Preview button on the Status bar, you might preview this page in the Print panel of the Backstage View and find that the printing is just too small to read comfortably. Go back to the Normal worksheet view, select the Page Layout tab on the Ribbon, and try changing the number of pages in the Width and Height drop-down menus in the Scale to Fit group.

Using the buttons in the Sheet Options group

The Sheet Options group contains two very useful Print check boxes (neither of which is selected automatically).

The first is in the Gridlines column, and the second is in the Headings column:

> ✔ Select the Print check box in the Gridlines column to print the column and row gridlines on each page of the report.

> ✔ Select the Print check box in the Headings column to print the row headings with the row numbers and the column headings with the column letters on each page of the report.

 Select both check boxes (by clicking them to put check marks in them) when you want the printed version of your spreadsheet data to closely match its onscreen appearance.

From Header to Footer

Headers and footers are simply standard text that appears on every page of the report. A header prints in the top margin of the page, and a footer prints — you guessed it — in the bottom margin. Both are centered vertically in the margins. Unless you specify otherwise, Excel does not automatically add either a header or footer to a new workbook.

The place to add a header or footer to a report is in Page Layout View. You can switch to this view by clicking the Page Layout View button on the Status bar.

When the worksheet is in Page Layout View, position the mouse pointer over the section in the top margin of the first page marked Click to Add Header or in the bottom margin of the first page marked Click to Add Footer.

To create a centered header or footer, click the center section of this header/footer area to set the insertion point in the middle of the section. To add a left-aligned header or footer, click the left section to set the insertion point flush with the left edge. To add a right-aligned header or footer, click the right section to set the insertion point flush with the right edge.

Immediately after setting the insertion point in the left, center, or right section of the header/footer area, Excel adds a Header & Footer Tools contextual tab with its own Design tab (see Figure 3-3). The Design tab is divided into Header & Footer, Header & Footer Elements, Navigation, and Options groups.

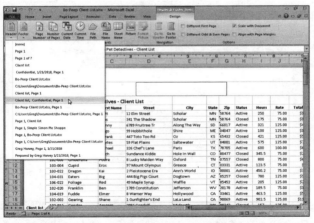

Figure 3-3: Defining a new header using the buttons on the Design tab of the Header & Footer Tools contextual tab.

54

Adding an Auto Header or Auto Footer

The Header and Footer command buttons on the Design tab of the Header & Footer Tools contextual tab enable you to add stock headers and footers in an instant. Simply click the appropriate command button and then click the header or footer example you want to use on the Header or Footer drop-down menu that appears.

To create the centered header and footer for the report in Figure 3-4, I selected Client List, Confidential, Page 1 on the Header command button's drop-down menu. Client List is the name of the worksheet, Confidential is stock text, and Page 1 is, of course, the current page number.

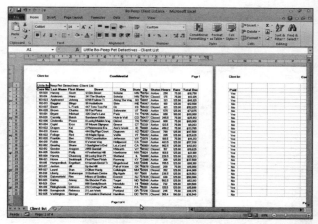

Figure 3-4: The first page of a report in Page Layout View shows you how the header and footer will print.

To set up the footer, I chose Page 1 of ? in the Footer command button's drop-down menu (which puts the current page number with the total number of pages in the report). You can select this paging option on either the Header or Footer button's drop-down menu.

Creating a custom header or footer

Most of the time, the stock headers and footers available on the Header button's and Footer button's drop-down menus are sufficient for your report printing needs. Occasionally, however, you may want to insert information not available in these list boxes or in an arrangement that Excel doesn't offer in the ready-made headers and footers.

For those times, you need to use the command buttons that appear in the Header & Footer Elements group of the Design tab on the Header & Footer Tools contextual tab. These command buttons enable you to blend your own information with that generated by Excel into different sections of the custom header or footer you're creating.

Solving Page Break Problems

The Page Break preview feature in Excel enables you to spot and fix page break problems in an instant, such as when the program wants to split information across different pages that you know should always be on the same page.

Figure 3-5 shows a worksheet in Page Break Preview with an example of a bad vertical page break that you can remedy by adjusting the location of the page break on Page 1 and Page 3. Given the page size, orientation, and margin settings for this report, Excel breaks the page between columns K and L. This break separates the Paid column (L) from all the others in the client list, effectively putting this information on its own Page 3 and Page 4 (not shown in Figure 3-5).

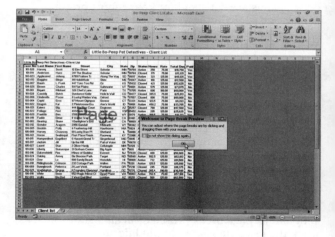

Page Break Preview

Figure 3-5: Preview page breaks in a report with Page Break Preview.

To prevent the data in the Paid column from printing on its own pages, you need to move the page break to a column on the left. In this case, I moved the page break to between columns G (with the zip code data) and H (containing the account status information) so that the name and address information stays together on Page 1 and Page 2 and the other client data is printed together on Page 3 and Page 4.

Figure 3-6 shows vertical page breaks in the Page Break Preview worksheet view, which you can accomplish by following these steps:

1. **Click the Page Break Preview button (refer to Figure 3-5).**

   This takes you into a Page Break Preview worksheet view that shows your worksheet data at a reduced magnification (60 percent of normal in Figure 3-6) with the page numbers displayed in large light type and the page breaks shown by heavy lines between the columns and rows of the worksheet.

2. **If the Welcome to Page Break Preview alert dialog box appears (refer to Figure 3-5), click OK to get rid of it.**

3. **Position the mouse pointer somewhere on the page break indicator (one of the heavy lines surrounding the representation of the page) that you need to adjust; when the pointer changes to a double-headed arrow, drag the page indicator to the desired column or row and release the mouse button.**

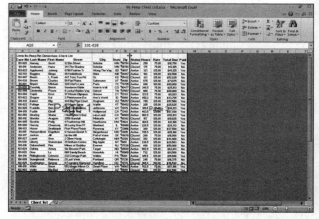

Figure 3-6: Page 1 of the report after adjusting the page breaks in the Page Break Preview worksheet view.

For the example shown in Figure 3-6, I dragged the page break indicator between Page 1 and Page 3 to the left so that it's between columns G and H. Excel placed the page break at this point, which puts all the name and address information together on Page 1 and Page 2. This new page break then causes all the other columns of client data to print together on Page 3 and Page 4.

4. **After you finish adjusting the page breaks in
   Page Break Preview (and, presumably, printing
   the report), click the Normal button (the first
   one in the cluster to the left of the Zoom slider)
   to return the worksheet to its regular view of the
   data.**

 You can also insert your own manual page
breaks at the cell cursor's position by clicking
Insert Page Break on the Breaks button's
drop-down menu on the Page Layout tab and
remove them by clicking Remove Page Break
on this menu.